WHAT OTHERS ARE SAYING

"I'm so enjoying my journaling, anticipating daily what God has in store for me. I have noticed a craving for reading my Bible more, listening to podcasts, and talking to people about what God is doing in my life. I can't seem to get away from, "Where do I see God?" and God telling me to be still and rest in His presence, stop being busy. Relax, relax, relax. I don't need to always be doing something." -*Judi*

"I felt like when I took the time to listen, God was often encouraging any uneasy thoughts I had that day. If I was stressing about something, I was prompted by God to give it up, and to be reminded of all He does to protect and guide me." -*Sarah*

"I was more aware of His presence and interactions in my daily routine. I was watching for what He was asking me to let go and to receive... where I saw Him in the details of my daily life. Most importantly, I was focused on where I could partner with Him that specific day." -*Lisa*

"This journal helped me carve out time in my day to talk to God through writing, reflecting and praying. I ended up talking with him more and reflecting about what I had written throughout my day. I did find myself talking to God more often, too. I started driving to work without music on and used this as quiet time to talk with God." -*Edie*

"I definitely listened to God more while using the I Am Listening Journal, which was beautiful. I love to talk so carving out space to listen for longer than a minute or two was always a challenge...and still is! But this motivated me to set aside that time because I wanted to write it down... and then going back to see how the themes were coming together. That catalyzed my motivation even further." -*Dr. Angel*

"This journal impacted how often I listened to God. I feel that I talk to God all the time but I don't always remember to listen." -*Jessica*

"The I Am Listening Journal was helpful for me. I was seeking a way to be closer to God. This "forced" (in a good way) me to dedicate 5-10 minutes a day to talking to him and being mindful. I also began to see God in people and in myself - this was eye-opening for me. I know He is with me and in me but that doesn't normally "click" - it was a cool discovery." - *Gina*

"I found myself listening to God more frequently while using this journal. It helped me to focus in on Him and not myself as much as usual." - *Jill*

"I used to speak with God daily for prayer, but actually listening was not happening much. I would thank God frequently, and then I would ask for things without really asking what He would like for me. This resource has opened up a whole new dialogue, and I feel like I can actually hear Him better. I am so incredibly blessed and thankful for this journal. I used to not know what to write about, not know what to say, and not know where to begin. This journal gave me the prompts to start my writing, but then opened up communication with God during the day when I would find myself facing various situations. It was a game and life changer!" - *Danielle*

"This practice made me feel more connected to God throughout the day. Sometimes He spoke at different times of the day, not just during my morning quiet time. I listened and I heard more, so that made me want to listen more! I felt like my steps were more aligned with His will. I felt more peace, and I had the desire to read more scripture!" - *Stephanie*

"I talk to God all the time throughout the day, but mostly I talk, and I don't stay still enough to listen! By journaling this way, I spent time quietly searching my heart, and waiting for God to nudge me. Being more aware of what wasn't serving me well (attitude, worry, etc), absolutely made a difference in my days. I MADE the time to listen. I didn't rush through it like a to-do list. I have to say it made my days more peaceful and joyful." - *Pam*

A WORD FROM THE AUTHOR
WHY GUIDED JOURNALING?

What joy it brings me to know you are embarking on this "I Am Listening" journey. The journal you hold in your hands is filled with few remarks from me; a fact that may come as a surprise to those who know I am never short on words. But the pages in this journal? They are for you and God to fill and that's the best kind of story.

As someone who discovered a love for writing and journaling fifteen plus years ago, I had no idea what I was missing until I began my own personal "I Am Listening" pilgrimage. Up until this past year, I had only used blank journals. In the beginning, during those seasons of my life where confusion and hurt clung to my chest like a wet blanket, I was especially prone to "spilling the beans of my heart" onto the page. This often meant writing out the play-by-play of how I had been sliced, diced, and every offense taken. In looking back at some of my first journals, it's no wonder I had such dis-ease, pervasive anxiety, and depression. While there is something cathartic and helpful to non-prompted writing, I now see how my free-flow thoughts were focused on the negative. Writing those thoughts day in and day out was doing nothing to help me get unstuck. I guess that's all I knew to do at the time, which brings up a super fun aspect I simply love about journaling - **documentation of growth.** Undoubtedly, you will look back at this journal and see the places where God carried you, the times of trial, of trust, joy and delight.

As the years went on and I grew in my faith and dependence on the Lord, my journal turned more into a space for gratitude. Prayers written to God became the norm. Dreams and goals also permeated those blank pages. And then...this gift of guided journaling came through a most unsuspecting place...I was asked to speak to a room full of mommas on Hearing From God. It was in preparation for that talk that I realized something: **my most transformational and treasured journal entries were the ones where I had asked God questions.** I would literally write the questions in my journal, sit and wait, often eyes closed, and listen. I'd write down whatever was placed on my heart in those moments. These entries were so pivotal to me that I photocopied them and taped them up in frequented places. (Yes, the potty room. I plastered my conversation with God about leaving my elementary teaching career next to the toilet. Let's just say I drink a lot of water so I knew I'd see it there - often.) As I continued to prep my talk for the mommas, I realized I had only done this "written conversation with God" a couple of times. Why? If the times I did were so powerful, why didn't I do it more often?

Around the same time I was making this discovery, the Lord was asking me to create more margin in my days - "Spend more time BEING with me." It was then He revealed something about my current habits:

READ DEVO QUICKLY-WRITE A FEW THOUGHTS IN JOURNAL-MOVE ON

I was DOING really great things. I was reading ABOUT Him and writing TO Him - both of which have their place. But, many times, neither of these actions left me feeling like I had spent time WITH Him. Jesus is LIVING WATER and yet, after my "quiet time" with Him, I often left with mouth still parched and thirsty for something more.

Add to this, I was navigating painful interactions with loved ones. Thankfully, I reached out to a spiritual mentor and friend who woke me up to **LISTENING** to the Holy Spirit again. I had gotten entrenched in lies and my ears were having a difficult time separating truth from falsity. Chances are, you're familiar with this kind of crud entering your thoughts: "You're not enough. All you'll ever be is a mistake." Ouch. I asked the Lord how to help prevent these weeds from rooting into my heart in the first place:

LISTEN TO ME, DEAR ONE. SPEND TIME WITH ME. HEAR MY VOICE.

It's a concept simple in nature, yet often made difficult in our full-speed-ahead, go-go-go world. It was then that I intentionally began creating time to listen. Naturally, the "I Am Listening Journal" was born from that obedience. Though indecision and fear had bogged me down for months, it took only days of listening and responding in my journal to exude more peace in my heart. Using the tool you now hold in your hands, I discovered a newfound joy in my soul as I began connecting with the Lord in a deeper way.

God is love. His love for us goes beyond measure. Intimacy with Him is the absolute most life-giving thing we could ever hope for and it's ours for the taking. I pray and hope and believe your time spent listening to the Holy Spirit in the following pages will be life-altering. May you let His words and His truths touch your heart, heal your hurts, and put a love so fierce and fiery inside of you that no amount of anything else can bring you down.

xo,

Tammy

Tips ON HOW TO USE THIS JOURNAL

I realize not everyone was born with a pen in their hand and a penchant for writing. In fact, you may only have this journal in your hands because someone else had a hunch you would benefit from it. (Thank God for the considerate people in our lives.) Whether you're reading these pages because you are eager to connect with the Lord or you thought this book was something else entirely - WELCOME. It's about to get fun up in here!

On the following pages, you're going to encounter an invitation to interact with the Holy Spirit. Invite Him in with prayer and continue the conversation with a series of eight guiding questions and prompts. I aim to get myself in an environment that's quiet(er), preferably first thing in the morning (I am a morning person though). I've had no other option but a busy airport at night and the Lord still showed up to meet me. You will notice there are prompts that feel more like prayer, such as offering up gratitude and giving praise for all the people, places, and spaces you see God in. There are also prompts which call us to be still and listen for Him to fill in the blanks. Enjoy the extra space at the end of every seven days to jot reflections from the week. Last, but not least, don't miss the At-A-Glance pages upon completion of your 40th day; designed to provide you with a snapshot of this season in your life. Because, when God is talking to you and walking with you, those are things to remember.

My biggest hope for all who use this journal is that they would be uplifted, encouraged, challenged, and able to feel the love of our Heavenly Father. What I'm realizing is, whatever you believe about the character of God, that's going to come through in your hearing from Him. If you think He's a brow-beater, never satisfied, angry sort of dad, you're probably going to hear something different than the one who believes God is gentle and kind. If you believe God is more concerned with your DOING than He is with your BEING, what you hear from Him will likely be a reflection of those beliefs. Be aware of this and, perhaps part of your journaling process will be asking God more about himself, too. What pure joy it would bring if, in spending this regular time talking with the Lord, it helped you develop a deeper and richer understanding of God and His character.

The hope I have for myself is to write in this every single day. While that hasn't exactly happened, something else has...on the one-off days where I haven't made the time to hop in here, I feel off. Instead of just accepting that all day long, I pause and ask the Lord a question or two from this journal - wherever I am. He meets me there, in that space, every time. Using this resource as a framework to slow down and listen has made THE difference in my life and relationship with the Lord. I hope you find it does the same for you.

Might you be thinking...Uhhhh...this sounds great and all, but what do I write? I am not here to dictate what you write. But after sharing this journal format with a few friends, the question did come up. Their feedback helped me see that sharing a few examples is helpful. If you're a free-thinker, a chart-the-course, then let me do my own thing sort of person, you can skip over the next few pages. Seriously. Don't even sneak a peek. The sample pages from my journal are merely here to give you an idea of what could transpire. Yours will look different. Celebrate that. Just as no two people have the same thumbprint, neither would our conversations with the Lord be matchy-matchy

If you do take a look at the following journal entries, note the voice. The first two questions may activate more of your mind (the place where most people camp out). The remaining questions are meant to draw you and the Holy Spirit in unity; a dependence on Him to garner the response.

Last but not least, be sure to enjoy the bonus coloring page at the end of every week. They are scripture-focused and filled with truth. Knowing scripture changes us. The way I see it, time spent on these pages can't help but commit them to memory. What a gift that will be to have life-giving words filling our minds.

A peek into my journal...

Date 5 / 28 / 19

Today I am grateful for *mentors in my life, the ability to move my body, the sun, your grace, second chances*

I see God In *flowers, birds chirping, my marriage, rest, creation, my ability to create new*

1 Am Listening - A Prayer

Holy Spirit,

You are welcome here.
I believe you care about me and long to comfort me.
I need your loving guidance in my life; I can't do it on my own.

I praise God that He designed it this way; Him, the Father,
the giver of life, His son, Jesus, imparted to set us free, and you,
the Holy Spirit, to be an ever-present help in times of need.

I invite you into my successes and into my messes.
I invite you into my relationships and into every time I trip.
I invite you into my pain and I invite you to remain.

Truth is - you have been and are there for it all anyway.

Holy Spirit, this week...this day...this hour...this minute...

I AM LISTENING.

Lord, what are our priorities today? finish writing devotional and send to a few women to get feedback. Send invitations to Noonday party, dinner w/ Bryan

Who are we praying for? The Dream House. Ed + Mary Kintz, The B Team and their families, those caught in Sex trafficking, all marriages

What truth do you have for me today, Lord? have fun, don't let fear make your decisions, be bold in pursuit of who I made you to be.

What do I need to let go of? figuring it all out. perfectionistic tendencies and being too strict with yourself - enjoy moments of spontaneity, too.

What do I need to receive? my abundant joy, trust and follow what I put in your heart, security in me - not in $, your weight... In me.

Lord, how can I partner with you today? Believe. Act on these beliefs. Keep stepping out. Know that you are worthy of great things. Keep listening.

COMMONLY ASKED QUESTIONS

Q: What if it feels weird to do this? To talk to the Lord and expect to hear from Him in return? I feel kinda silly.
A: The Lord encourages us in His word to have childlike belief and humility. I haven't met a child yet who didn't ask questions and long for an answer. Feel silly. Honestly, it's good for you. That's a part of intimacy, too - putting yourself out there. Let pride take a backseat while you usher humility and boldness in.

Q: How do I know it's Him and not just me writing what I want to hear?
A: Great question. If what you are hearing from the Lord in any way does not line up with the Bible, press pause. The Holy Spirit will never contradict God's Word. You will likely feel disagreement in the pit of your stomach. A knowing. Another way to help decipher? Seek Godly counsel. A trusted Christ-follower can help you see things clearly, too. One way I often know it's God speaking to me is that it doesn't sound like my own internal thoughts. He often gives me words that are so full of kindness and compassion they leave me teary-eyed. (That being said, the more I practice this guided journal time with the Lord, the more I notice my thoughts being in agreement with HIS words and thoughts about me - victory!)

Q: Should I be hearing an actual audible voice?
A: You may. You may not. More often than not, you will not. My experience has been more of an internal knowing, a heart knowledge that rises to the surface when called upon. It brings peace and strength. Even when the Spirit is speaking into my disobedience or waking me to take action on something, it's never belittling or degrading.

Q: Is this journal meant for people who are new in their faith or those who've known God for decades?
A: Yes. All of the above and beyond. I believe God can use these prompts, these pages, this practice of getting still and listening, with anyone and everyone. The details do not matter. Your oneness with God does.

Q: What do I do with what I hear?
A: Start by writing it in your journal so you can refer back. This will allow you to look for themes and notice where you're hearing the same things repeatedly. What if the Lord whispers something to you that isn't what you think you want to hear? Aka - it gets you out of your comfort zone and goes against the "perfect plan" you had in mind. In this situation, you may want to convince yourself it was not really God you heard from. Note, you

would not be the first person to do this. If you find yourself in that circumstance, I encourage you to lean in. Be direct and ask God to give you clarity. Listen for like-minded messages. Do you get similar learnings from your Bible study time? Does a teaching in church reiterate what you wrote in this journal? If your ears are sensitive, you will often get confirmation in other places. Best thing to do with what you hear?

Trust Him. Take action.
Where God guides, He provides.

It's time.

He's ready.

*Open your heart
and LISTEN.*

Today I am grateful for _____

_____

_____

_____

I see God In _____

_____

_____

_____

I Am Listening - A Prayer

Holy Spirit,

You are welcome here.
I believe you care about me and long to comfort me.
I need your loving guidance in my life; I can't do it on my own.

I praise God that He designed it this way; Him, the Father,
the giver of life, His son, Jesus, imparted to set us free, and you,
the Holy Spirit, to be an ever-present help in times of need.

I invite you into my successes and into my messes.
I invite you into my relationships and into every time I trip.
I invite you into my pain and I invite you to remain.

Truth is - you have been and are there for it all anyway.

Holy Spirit, this week...this day...this hour...this minute...

I AM LISTENING.

Lord, what are our priorities today?

_____

_____

_____

Who are we praying for?

_____

_____

_____

What truth do you have for me today, Lord?

_____

_____

_____

What do I need to let go of?

_____

_____

_____

What do I need to receive?

_____

_____

_____

Lord, how can I partner with you today?

_____

_____

Today I am grateful for _____

_____

_____

_____

I see God In _____

_____

_____

_____

I Am Listening - A Prayer

Holy Spirit,

You are welcome here.
I believe you care about me and long to comfort me.
I need your loving guidance in my life; I can't do it on my own.

I praise God that He designed it this way; Him, the Father,
the giver of life, His son, Jesus, imparted to set us free, and you,
the Holy Spirit, to be an ever-present help in times of need.

I invite you into my successes and into my messes.
I invite you into my relationships and into every time I trip.
I invite you into my pain and I invite you to remain.

Truth is - you have been and are there for it all anyway.

Holy Spirit, this week...this day...this hour...this minute...

I AM LISTENING.

Lord, what are our priorities today?

_____

_____

_____

Who are we praying for?

_____

_____

_____

What truth do you have for me today, Lord?

_____

_____

_____

What do I need to let go of?

_____

_____

_____

What do I need to receive?

_____

_____

_____

Lord, how can I partner with you today?

_____

_____

Date ____ / ____ / ____

Today I am grateful for _____

_____

_____

_____

I see God In _____

_____

_____

_____

I Am Listening - A Prayer

Holy Spirit,

You are welcome here.
I believe you care about me and long to comfort me.
I need your loving guidance in my life; I can't do it on my own.

I praise God that He designed it this way; Him, the Father,
the giver of life, His son, Jesus, imparted to set us free, and you,
the Holy Spirit, to be an ever-present help in times of need.

I invite you into my successes and into my messes.
I invite you into my relationships and into every time I trip.
I invite you into my pain and I invite you to remain.

Truth is - you have been and are there for it all anyway.

Holy Spirit, this week...this day...this hour...this minute...

I AM LISTENING.

Lord, what are our priorities today? _____

_____

_____

_____

Who are we praying for? _____

_____

_____

_____

What truth do you have for me today, Lord? _____

_____

_____

_____

What do I need to let go of? _____

_____

_____

_____

What do I need to receive? _____

_____

_____

_____

Lord, how can I partner with you today? _____

_____

_____

Today I am grateful for _____

_____

_____

_____

I see God In _____

_____

_____

_____

I Am Listening - A Prayer

Holy Spirit,

You are welcome here.
I believe you care about me and long to comfort me.
I need your loving guidance in my life; I can't do it on my own.

I praise God that He designed it this way; Him, the Father,
the giver of life, His son, Jesus, imparted to set us free, and you,
the Holy Spirit, to be an ever-present help in times of need.

I invite you into my successes and into my messes.
I invite you into my relationships and into every time I trip.
I invite you into my pain and I invite you to remain.

Truth is - you have been and are there for it all anyway.

Holy Spirit, this week...this day...this hour...this minute...

I AM LISTENING.

Lord, what are our priorities today? _____

_____

_____

_____

Who are we praying for? _____

_____

_____

_____

What truth do you have for me today, Lord? _____

_____

_____

_____

What do I need to let go of? _____

_____

_____

_____

What do I need to receive? _____

_____

_____

_____

Lord, how can I partner with you today? _____

_____

_____

Today I am grateful for _____

_____

_____

_____

I see God In _____

_____

_____

_____

I Am Listening - A Prayer

Holy Spirit,

You are welcome here.
I believe you care about me and long to comfort me.
I need your loving guidance in my life; I can't do it on my own.

I praise God that He designed it this way; Him, the Father,
the giver of life, His son, Jesus, imparted to set us free, and you,
the Holy Spirit, to be an ever-present help in times of need.

I invite you into my successes and into my messes.
I invite you into my relationships and into every time I trip.
I invite you into my pain and I invite you to remain.

Truth is - you have been and are there for it all anyway.

Holy Spirit, this week...this day...this hour...this minute...

I AM LISTENING.

Lord, what are our priorities today? _____

_____

_____

_____

Who are we praying for? _____

_____

_____

_____

What truth do you have for me today, Lord? _____

_____

_____

_____

What do I need to let go of? _____

_____

_____

_____

What do I need to receive? _____

_____

_____

_____

Lord, how can I partner with you today? _____

_____

_____

Today I am grateful for _____

_____

_____

_____

_____

I see God In _____

_____

_____

_____

I Am Listening - A Prayer

Holy Spirit,

You are welcome here.
I believe you care about me and long to comfort me.
I need your loving guidance in my life; I can't do it on my own.

I praise God that He designed it this way; Him, the Father,
the giver of life, His son, Jesus, imparted to set us free, and you,
the Holy Spirit, to be an ever-present help in times of need.

I invite you into my successes and into my messes.
I invite you into my relationships and into every time I trip.
I invite you into my pain and I invite you to remain.

Truth is - you have been and are there for it all anyway.

Holy Spirit, this week...this day...this hour...this minute...

I AM LISTENING.

Lord, what are our priorities today? _____

_____

_____

_____

Who are we praying for? _____

_____

_____

_____

What truth do you have for me today, Lord? _____

_____

_____

_____

What do I need to let go of? _____

_____

_____

_____

What do I need to receive? _____

_____

_____

_____

Lord, how can I partner with you today? _____

_____

_____

Today I am grateful for _____

_____

_____

_____

I see God In _____

_____

_____

_____

I Am Listening - A Prayer

Holy Spirit,

You are welcome here.
I believe you care about me and long to comfort me.
I need your loving guidance in my life; I can't do it on my own.

I praise God that He designed it this way; Him, the Father,
the giver of life, His son, Jesus, imparted to set us free, and you,
the Holy Spirit, to be an ever-present help in times of need.

I invite you into my successes and into my messes.
I invite you into my relationships and into every time I trip.
I invite you into my pain and I invite you to remain.

Truth is - you have been and are there for it all anyway.

Holy Spirit, this week...this day...this hour...this minute...

I AM LISTENING.

Lord, what are our priorities today? _____

_____

_____

_____

Who are we praying for? _____

_____

_____

_____

What truth do you have for me today, Lord? _____

_____

_____

_____

What do I need to let go of? _____

_____

_____

_____

What do I need to receive? _____

_____

_____

_____

Lord, how can I partner with you today? _____

_____

_____

Weekly Reflections

Did any themes emerge in your listening this week? What are the ways you saw God? Evidence the Holy Spirit is growing you? Anything else you want to remember from the week?

DON'T YOU
KNOW THAT YOU
YOURSELVES ARE

God's Temple

AND THAT
GOD'S SPIRIT

dwells

IN YOUR MIDST?

1 CORINTHIANS 3:16 NIV

Date ____ / ____ / ____

Today I am grateful for _____

_____

_____

_____

I see God In _____

_____

_____

_____

7 Am Listening - A Prayer

Holy Spirit,

You are welcome here.
I believe you care about me and long to comfort me.
I need your loving guidance in my life; I can't do it on my own.

I praise God that He designed it this way; Him, the Father,
the giver of life, His son, Jesus, imparted to set us free, and you,
the Holy Spirit, to be an ever-present help in times of need.

I invite you into my successes and into my messes.
I invite you into my relationships and into every time I trip.
I invite you into my pain and I invite you to remain.

Truth is - you have been and are there for it all anyway.

Holy Spirit, this week...this day...this hour...this minute...

I AM LISTENING.

Lord, what are our priorities today? _____

_____

_____

_____

Who are we praying for? _____

_____

_____

_____

What truth do you have for me today, Lord? _____

_____

_____

_____

What do I need to let go of? _____

_____

_____

_____

What do I need to receive? _____

_____

_____

_____

Lord, how can I partner with you today? _____

_____

_____

Today I am grateful for _____

_____

_____

_____

I see God In _____

_____

_____

_____

I Am Listening - A Prayer

Holy Spirit,

You are welcome here.
I believe you care about me and long to comfort me.
I need your loving guidance in my life; I can't do it on my own.

I praise God that He designed it this way; Him, the Father,
the giver of life, His son, Jesus, imparted to set us free, and you,
the Holy Spirit, to be an ever-present help in times of need.

I invite you into my successes and into my messes.
I invite you into my relationships and into every time I trip.
I invite you into my pain and I invite you to remain.

Truth is - you have been and are there for it all anyway.

Holy Spirit, this week...this day...this hour...this minute...

I AM LISTENING.

Lord, what are our priorities today?

_____

_____

_____

Who are we praying for?

_____

_____

_____

What truth do you have for me today, Lord?

_____

_____

_____

What do I need to let go of?

_____

_____

_____

What do I need to receive?

_____

_____

_____

Lord, how can I partner with you today?

_____

_____

Date _____ / _____ / _____

Today I am grateful for _____

_____

_____

_____

I see God In _____

_____

_____

_____

1 Am Listening - A Prayer

Holy Spirit,

You are welcome here.
I believe you care about me and long to comfort me.
I need your loving guidance in my life; I can't do it on my own.

I praise God that He designed it this way; Him, the Father,
the giver of life, His son, Jesus, imparted to set us free, and you,
the Holy Spirit, to be an ever-present help in times of need.

I invite you into my successes and into my messes.
I invite you into my relationships and into every time I trip.
I invite you into my pain and I invite you to remain.

Truth is - you have been and are there for it all anyway.

Holy Spirit, this week...this day...this hour...this minute...

I AM LISTENING.

Lord, what are our priorities today? _____

_____

_____

_____

Who are we praying for? _____

_____

_____

_____

What truth do you have for me today, Lord? _____

_____

_____

_____

What do I need to let go of? _____

_____

_____

_____

What do I need to receive? _____

_____

_____

_____

Lord, how can I partner with you today? _____

_____

_____

Date ____ / ____ / ____

Today I am grateful for _____

_____

_____

_____

I see God In _____

_____

_____

_____

I Am Listening - A Prayer

Holy Spirit,

You are welcome here.
I believe you care about me and long to comfort me.
I need your loving guidance in my life; I can't do it on my own.

I praise God that He designed it this way; Him, the Father,
the giver of life, His son, Jesus, imparted to set us free, and you,
the Holy Spirit, to be an ever-present help in times of need.

I invite you into my successes and into my messes.
I invite you into my relationships and into every time I trip.
I invite you into my pain and I invite you to remain.

Truth is - you have been and are there for it all anyway.

Holy Spirit, this week...this day...this hour...this minute...

I AM LISTENING.

Lord, what are our priorities today? _____

_____

_____

_____

Who are we praying for? _____

_____

_____

_____

What truth do you have for me today, Lord? _____

_____

_____

_____

What do I need to let go of? _____

_____

_____

_____

What do I need to receive? _____

_____

_____

_____

Lord, how can I partner with you today? _____

_____

_____

Today I am grateful for _____

_____

_____

_____

I see God In _____

_____

_____

_____

I Am Listening - A Prayer

Holy Spirit,

You are welcome here.
I believe you care about me and long to comfort me.
I need your loving guidance in my life; I can't do it on my own.

I praise God that He designed it this way; Him, the Father,
the giver of life, His son, Jesus, imparted to set us free, and you,
the Holy Spirit, to be an ever-present help in times of need.

I invite you into my successes and into my messes.
I invite you into my relationships and into every time I trip.
I invite you into my pain and I invite you to remain.

Truth is - you have been and are there for it all anyway.

Holy Spirit, this week...this day...this hour...this minute...

I AM LISTENING.

Lord, what are our priorities today? _____

_____

_____

_____

Who are we praying for? _____

_____

_____

_____

What truth do you have for me today, Lord? _____

_____

_____

_____

What do I need to let go of? _____

_____

_____

_____

What do I need to receive? _____

_____

_____

_____

Lord, how can I partner with you today? _____

_____

_____

Today I am grateful for _____

_____

_____

_____

I see God In _____

_____

_____

_____

I Am Listening - A Prayer

Holy Spirit,

You are welcome here.
I believe you care about me and long to comfort me.
I need your loving guidance in my life; I can't do it on my own.

I praise God that He designed it this way; Him, the Father,
the giver of life, His son, Jesus, imparted to set us free, and you,
the Holy Spirit, to be an ever-present help in times of need.

I invite you into my successes and into my messes.
I invite you into my relationships and into every time I trip.
I invite you into my pain and I invite you to remain.

Truth is - you have been and are there for it all anyway.

Holy Spirit, this week...this day...this hour...this minute...

I AM LISTENING.

Lord, what are our priorities today? _____

_____

_____

_____

Who are we praying for? _____

_____

_____

_____

What truth do you have for me today, Lord? _____

_____

_____

_____

What do I need to let go of? _____

_____

_____

_____

What do I need to receive? _____

_____

_____

_____

Lord, how can I partner with you today? _____

_____

_____

Date ____ / ____ / ____

Today I am grateful for _____

_____

_____

_____

I see God In _____

_____

_____

_____

I Am Listening - A Prayer

Holy Spirit,

You are welcome here.
I believe you care about me and long to comfort me.
I need your loving guidance in my life; I can't do it on my own.

I praise God that He designed it this way; Him, the Father,
the giver of life, His son, Jesus, imparted to set us free, and you,
the Holy Spirit, to be an ever-present help in times of need.

I invite you into my successes and into my messes.
I invite you into my relationships and into every time I trip.
I invite you into my pain and I invite you to remain.

Truth is - you have been and are there for it all anyway.

Holy Spirit, this week...this day...this hour...this minute...

I AM LISTENING.

Lord, what are our priorities today? _____

_____

_____

_____

Who are we praying for? _____

_____

_____

_____

What truth do you have for me today, Lord? _____

_____

_____

_____

What do I need to let go of? _____

_____

_____

_____

What do I need to receive? _____

_____

_____

_____

Lord, how can I partner with you today? _____

_____

_____

Weekly Reflections

Did any themes emerge in your listening this week? What are the ways you saw God? Evidence the Holy Spirit is growing you? Anything else you want to remember from the week?

TEACH ME TO DO YOUR WILL, FOR *you are my God;* MAY YOUR GOOD SPIRIT LEAD ME ON LEVEL GROUND.

PSALM 143:10 NIV

Today I am grateful for _____

_____

_____

_____

I see God In _____

_____

_____

_____

I Am Listening - A Prayer

Holy Spirit,

You are welcome here.
I believe you care about me and long to comfort me.
I need your loving guidance in my life; I can't do it on my own.

I praise God that He designed it this way; Him, the Father,
the giver of life, His son, Jesus, imparted to set us free, and you,
the Holy Spirit, to be an ever-present help in times of need.

I invite you into my successes and into my messes.
I invite you into my relationships and into every time I trip.
I invite you into my pain and I invite you to remain.

Truth is - you have been and are there for it all anyway.

Holy Spirit, this week...this day...this hour...this minute...

I AM LISTENING.

Lord, what are our priorities today? _____

_____

_____

_____

Who are we praying for? _____

_____

_____

_____

What truth do you have for me today, Lord? _____

_____

_____

_____

What do I need to let go of? _____

_____

_____

_____

What do I need to receive? _____

_____

_____

_____

Lord, how can I partner with you today? _____

_____

_____

Today I am grateful for _____

_____

_____

_____

I see God In _____

_____

_____

_____

I Am Listening - A Prayer

Holy Spirit,

You are welcome here.
I believe you care about me and long to comfort me.
I need your loving guidance in my life; I can't do it on my own.

I praise God that He designed it this way; Him, the Father,
the giver of life, His son, Jesus, imparted to set us free, and you,
the Holy Spirit, to be an ever-present help in times of need.

I invite you into my successes and into my messes.
I invite you into my relationships and into every time I trip.
I invite you into my pain and I invite you to remain.

Truth is - you have been and are there for it all anyway.

Holy Spirit, this week...this day...this hour...this minute...

I AM LISTENING.

Lord, what are our priorities today? _____

_____

_____

_____

Who are we praying for? _____

_____

_____

_____

What truth do you have for me today, Lord? _____

_____

_____

_____

What do I need to let go of? _____

_____

_____

_____

What do I need to receive? _____

_____

_____

_____

Lord, how can I partner with you today? _____

_____

_____

Date ____ / ____ / ____

Today I am grateful for _____

_____

_____

_____

I see God In _____

_____

_____

_____

I Am Listening - A Prayer

Holy Spirit,

You are welcome here.
I believe you care about me and long to comfort me.
I need your loving guidance in my life; I can't do it on my own.

I praise God that He designed it this way; Him, the Father,
the giver of life, His son, Jesus, imparted to set us free, and you,
the Holy Spirit, to be an ever-present help in times of need.

I invite you into my successes and into my messes.
I invite you into my relationships and into every time I trip.
I invite you into my pain and I invite you to remain.

Truth is - you have been and are there for it all anyway.

Holy Spirit, this week...this day...this hour...this minute...

I AM LISTENING.

Lord, what are our priorities today? _____

_____

_____

_____

Who are we praying for? _____

_____

_____

_____

What truth do you have for me today, Lord? _____

_____

_____

_____

What do I need to let go of? _____

_____

_____

_____

What do I need to receive? _____

_____

_____

_____

Lord, how can I partner with you today? _____

_____

_____

Today I am grateful for _____

_____

_____

_____

I see God In _____

_____

_____

_____

I Am Listening - A Prayer

Holy Spirit,

You are welcome here.
I believe you care about me and long to comfort me.
I need your loving guidance in my life; I can't do it on my own.

I praise God that He designed it this way; Him, the Father,
the giver of life, His son, Jesus, imparted to set us free, and you,
the Holy Spirit, to be an ever-present help in times of need.

I invite you into my successes and into my messes.
I invite you into my relationships and into every time I trip.
I invite you into my pain and I invite you to remain.

Truth is - you have been and are there for it all anyway.

Holy Spirit, this week...this day...this hour...this minute...

I AM LISTENING.

Lord, what are our priorities today? _____

_____

_____

_____

Who are we praying for? _____

_____

_____

_____

What truth do you have for me today, Lord? _____

_____

_____

_____

What do I need to let go of? _____

_____

_____

_____

What do I need to receive? _____

_____

_____

_____

Lord, how can I partner with you today? _____

_____

_____

Date ____ / ____ / ____

Today I am grateful for _____

_____

_____

_____

I see God In _____

_____

_____

_____

I Am Listening - A Prayer

Holy Spirit,

You are welcome here.
I believe you care about me and long to comfort me.
I need your loving guidance in my life; I can't do it on my own.

I praise God that He designed it this way; Him, the Father,
the giver of life, His son, Jesus, imparted to set us free, and you,
the Holy Spirit, to be an ever-present help in times of need.

I invite you into my successes and into my messes.
I invite you into my relationships and into every time I trip.
I invite you into my pain and I invite you to remain.

Truth is - you have been and are there for it all anyway.

Holy Spirit, this week...this day...this hour...this minute...

I AM LISTENING.

Lord, what are our priorities today? _____

_____

_____

_____

Who are we praying for? _____

_____

_____

_____

What truth do you have for me today, Lord? _____

_____

_____

_____

What do I need to let go of? _____

_____

_____

_____

What do I need to receive? _____

_____

_____

_____

Lord, how can I partner with you today? _____

_____

_____

Today I am grateful for _____

_____

_____

_____

I see God In _____

_____

_____

_____

I Am Listening - A Prayer

Holy Spirit,

You are welcome here.
I believe you care about me and long to comfort me.
I need your loving guidance in my life; I can't do it on my own.

I praise God that He designed it this way; Him, the Father,
the giver of life, His son, Jesus, imparted to set us free, and you,
the Holy Spirit, to be an ever-present help in times of need.

I invite you into my successes and into my messes.
I invite you into my relationships and into every time I trip.
I invite you into my pain and I invite you to remain.

Truth is - you have been and are there for it all anyway.

Holy Spirit, this week...this day...this hour...this minute...

I AM LISTENING.

Lord, what are our priorities today? _____

_____

_____

_____

Who are we praying for? _____

_____

_____

_____

What truth do you have for me today, Lord? _____

_____

_____

_____

What do I need to let go of? _____

_____

_____

_____

What do I need to receive? _____

_____

_____

_____

Lord, how can I partner with you today? _____

_____

_____

Today I am grateful for _____

_____

_____

_____

I see God In _____

_____

_____

_____

I Am Listening - A Prayer

Holy Spirit,

You are welcome here.
I believe you care about me and long to comfort me.
I need your loving guidance in my life; I can't do it on my own.

I praise God that He designed it this way; Him, the Father,
the giver of life, His son, Jesus, imparted to set us free, and you,
the Holy Spirit, to be an ever-present help in times of need.

I invite you into my successes and into my messes.
I invite you into my relationships and into every time I trip.
I invite you into my pain and I invite you to remain.

Truth is - you have been and are there for it all anyway.

Holy Spirit, this week...this day...this hour...this minute...

I AM LISTENING.

Lord, what are our priorities today? _____

_____

_____

_____

Who are we praying for? _____

_____

_____

_____

What truth do you have for me today, Lord? _____

_____

_____

_____

What do I need to let go of? _____

_____

_____

_____

What do I need to receive? _____

_____

_____

_____

Lord, how can I partner with you today? _____

_____

_____

Weekly Reflections

Did any themes emerge in your listening this week? What are the ways you saw God? Evidence the Holy Spirit is growing you? Anything else you want to remember from the week?

He saved us,
NOT BECAUSE OF
RIGHTEOUS THINGS
WE HAD DONE, BUT
*because of
His mercy.*
HE SAVED US
THROUGH THE
WASHING OF REBIRTH
AND RENEWAL BY
THE HOLY SPIRIT.

TITUS 3:5 NIV

Today I am grateful for _____

_____

_____

_____

I see God In _____

_____

_____

_____

I Am Listening - A Prayer

Holy Spirit,

You are welcome here.
I believe you care about me and long to comfort me.
I need your loving guidance in my life; I can't do it on my own.

I praise God that He designed it this way; Him, the Father,
the giver of life, His son, Jesus, imparted to set us free, and you,
the Holy Spirit, to be an ever-present help in times of need.

I invite you into my successes and into my messes.
I invite you into my relationships and into every time I trip.
I invite you into my pain and I invite you to remain.

Truth is - you have been and are there for it all anyway.

Holy Spirit, this week...this day...this hour...this minute...

I AM LISTENING.

Lord, what are our priorities today? _____

_____

_____

_____

Who are we praying for? _____

_____

_____

_____

What truth do you have for me today, Lord? _____

_____

_____

_____

What do I need to let go of? _____

_____

_____

_____

What do I need to receive? _____

_____

_____

_____

Lord, how can I partner with you today? _____

_____

_____

Today I am grateful for _____

_____

_____

_____

I see God In _____

_____

_____

_____

7 Am Listening - A Prayer

Holy Spirit,

You are welcome here.
I believe you care about me and long to comfort me.
I need your loving guidance in my life; I can't do it on my own.

I praise God that He designed it this way; Him, the Father,
the giver of life, His son, Jesus, imparted to set us free, and you,
the Holy Spirit, to be an ever-present help in times of need.

I invite you into my successes and into my messes.
I invite you into my relationships and into every time I trip.
I invite you into my pain and I invite you to remain.

Truth is - you have been and are there for it all anyway.

Holy Spirit, this week...this day...this hour...this minute...

I AM LISTENING.

Lord, what are our priorities today?

Who are we praying for?

What truth do you have for me today, Lord?

What do I need to let go of?

What do I need to receive?

Lord, how can I partner with you today?

Today I am grateful for _____

_____

_____

_____

I see God In _____

_____

_____

_____

I Am Listening - A Prayer

Holy Spirit,

You are welcome here.
I believe you care about me and long to comfort me.
I need your loving guidance in my life; I can't do it on my own.

I praise God that He designed it this way; Him, the Father,
the giver of life, His son, Jesus, imparted to set us free, and you,
the Holy Spirit, to be an ever-present help in times of need.

I invite you into my successes and into my messes.
I invite you into my relationships and into every time I trip.
I invite you into my pain and I invite you to remain.

Truth is - you have been and are there for it all anyway.

Holy Spirit, this week...this day...this hour...this minute...

I AM LISTENING.

Lord, what are our priorities today? _____

_____

_____

_____

Who are we praying for? _____

_____

_____

_____

What truth do you have for me today, Lord? _____

_____

_____

_____

What do I need to let go of? _____

_____

_____

_____

What do I need to receive? _____

_____

_____

_____

Lord, how can I partner with you today? _____

_____

_____

Today I am grateful for _____

_____

_____

_____

I see God In _____

_____

_____

_____

7 Am Listening - A Prayer

Holy Spirit,

You are welcome here.
I believe you care about me and long to comfort me.
I need your loving guidance in my life; I can't do it on my own.

I praise God that He designed it this way; Him, the Father,
the giver of life, His son, Jesus, imparted to set us free, and you,
the Holy Spirit, to be an ever-present help in times of need.

I invite you into my successes and into my messes.
I invite you into my relationships and into every time I trip.
I invite you into my pain and I invite you to remain.

Truth is - you have been and are there for it all anyway.

Holy Spirit, this week...this day...this hour...this minute...

I AM LISTENING.

Lord, what are our priorities today? _____

_____

_____

_____

Who are we praying for? _____

_____

_____

_____

What truth do you have for me today, Lord? _____

_____

_____

_____

What do I need to let go of? _____

_____

_____

_____

What do I need to receive? _____

_____

_____

_____

Lord, how can I partner with you today? _____

_____

_____

Today I am grateful for _____

_____

_____

_____

I see God In _____

_____

_____

_____

I Am Listening - A Prayer

Holy Spirit,

You are welcome here.
I believe you care about me and long to comfort me.
I need your loving guidance in my life; I can't do it on my own.

I praise God that He designed it this way; Him, the Father,
the giver of life, His son, Jesus, imparted to set us free, and you,
the Holy Spirit, to be an ever-present help in times of need.

I invite you into my successes and into my messes.
I invite you into my relationships and into every time I trip.
I invite you into my pain and I invite you to remain.

Truth is - you have been and are there for it all anyway.

Holy Spirit, this week...this day...this hour...this minute...

I AM LISTENING.

Lord, what are our priorities today? _____

_____

_____

_____

Who are we praying for? _____

_____

_____

_____

What truth do you have for me today, Lord? _____

_____

_____

What do I need to let go of? _____

_____

_____

What do I need to receive? _____

_____

_____

Lord, how can I partner with you today? _____

_____

_____

Today I am grateful for _____

_____

_____

_____

I see God In _____

_____

_____

_____

I Am Listening - A Prayer

Holy Spirit,

You are welcome here.
I believe you care about me and long to comfort me.
I need your loving guidance in my life; I can't do it on my own.

I praise God that He designed it this way; Him, the Father,
the giver of life, His son, Jesus, imparted to set us free, and you,
the Holy Spirit, to be an ever-present help in times of need.

I invite you into my successes and into my messes.
I invite you into my relationships and into every time I trip.
I invite you into my pain and I invite you to remain.

Truth is - you have been and are there for it all anyway.

Holy Spirit, this week...this day...this hour...this minute...

I AM LISTENING.

Lord, what are our priorities today? _____

_____

_____

_____

Who are we praying for? _____

_____

_____

_____

What truth do you have for me today, Lord? _____

_____

_____

_____

What do I need to let go of? _____

_____

_____

_____

What do I need to receive? _____

_____

_____

_____

Lord, how can I partner with you today? _____

_____

_____

_____

Date ___ / ___ / ___

Today I am grateful for _____

_____

_____

_____

I see God In _____

_____

_____

_____

I Am Listening - A Prayer

Holy Spirit,

You are welcome here.
I believe you care about me and long to comfort me.
I need your loving guidance in my life; I can't do it on my own.

I praise God that He designed it this way; Him, the Father,
the giver of life, His son, Jesus, imparted to set us free, and you,
the Holy Spirit, to be an ever-present help in times of need.

I invite you into my successes and into my messes.
I invite you into my relationships and into every time I trip.
I invite you into my pain and I invite you to remain.

Truth is - you have been and are there for it all anyway.

Holy Spirit, this week...this day...this hour...this minute...

I AM LISTENING.

Lord, what are our priorities today? _____

_____

_____

_____

Who are we praying for? _____

_____

_____

_____

What truth do you have for me today, Lord? _____

_____

_____

_____

What do I need to let go of? _____

_____

_____

_____

What do I need to receive? _____

_____

_____

_____

Lord, how can I partner with you today? _____

_____

_____

Weekly Reflections

Did any themes emerge in your listening this week? What are the ways you saw God? Evidence the Holy Spirit is growing you? Anything else you want to remember from the week?

NOW THE LORD IS THE SPIRIT, AND WHERE THE SPIRIT OF THE LORD IS,

there is liberty

[EMANCIPATION FROM BONDAGE,

true freedom].

2 CORINTHIANS 3:17 AMP

Today I am grateful for _____

_____

_____

_____

I see God In _____

_____

_____

_____

I Am Listening - A Prayer

Holy Spirit,

You are welcome here.
I believe you care about me and long to comfort me.
I need your loving guidance in my life; I can't do it on my own.

I praise God that He designed it this way; Him, the Father,
the giver of life, His son, Jesus, imparted to set us free, and you,
the Holy Spirit, to be an ever-present help in times of need.

I invite you into my successes and into my messes.
I invite you into my relationships and into every time I trip.
I invite you into my pain and I invite you to remain.

Truth is - you have been and are there for it all anyway.

Holy Spirit, this week...this day...this hour...this minute...

I AM LISTENING.

Lord, what are our priorities today? _____

_____

_____

_____

Who are we praying for? _____

_____

_____

_____

What truth do you have for me today, Lord? _____

_____

_____

_____

What do I need to let go of? _____

_____

_____

_____

What do I need to receive? _____

_____

_____

_____

Lord, how can I partner with you today? _____

_____

_____

Today I am grateful for _____

_____

_____

_____

I see God In _____

_____

_____

_____

I Am Listening - A Prayer

Holy Spirit,

You are welcome here.
I believe you care about me and long to comfort me.
I need your loving guidance in my life; I can't do it on my own.

I praise God that He designed it this way; Him, the Father,
the giver of life, His son, Jesus, imparted to set us free, and you,
the Holy Spirit, to be an ever-present help in times of need.

I invite you into my successes and into my messes.
I invite you into my relationships and into every time I trip.
I invite you into my pain and I invite you to remain.

Truth is - you have been and are there for it all anyway.

Holy Spirit, this week...this day...this hour...this minute...

I AM LISTENING.

Lord, what are our priorities today? _____

_____

_____

_____

Who are we praying for? _____

_____

_____

_____

What truth do you have for me today, Lord? _____

_____

_____

_____

What do I need to let go of? _____

_____

_____

_____

What do I need to receive? _____

_____

_____

_____

Lord, how can I partner with you today? _____

_____

_____

Today I am grateful for _____

_____

_____

_____

I see God In _____

_____

_____

_____

I Am Listening - A Prayer

Holy Spirit,

You are welcome here.
I believe you care about me and long to comfort me.
I need your loving guidance in my life; I can't do it on my own.

I praise God that He designed it this way; Him, the Father,
the giver of life, His son, Jesus, imparted to set us free, and you,
the Holy Spirit, to be an ever-present help in times of need.

I invite you into my successes and into my messes.
I invite you into my relationships and into every time I trip.
I invite you into my pain and I invite you to remain.

Truth is - you have been and are there for it all anyway.

Holy Spirit, this week...this day...this hour...this minute...

I AM LISTENING.

Lord, what are our priorities today? _____

_____

_____

_____

Who are we praying for? _____

_____

_____

_____

What truth do you have for me today, Lord? _____

_____

_____

_____

What do I need to let go of? _____

_____

_____

_____

What do I need to receive? _____

_____

_____

_____

Lord, how can I partner with you today? _____

_____

_____

Date _____ / _____ / _____

Today I am grateful for _____

_____

_____

_____

I see God In _____

_____

_____

_____

I Am Listening - A Prayer

Holy Spirit,

You are welcome here.
I believe you care about me and long to comfort me.
I need your loving guidance in my life; I can't do it on my own.

I praise God that He designed it this way; Him, the Father,
the giver of life, His son, Jesus, imparted to set us free, and you,
the Holy Spirit, to be an ever-present help in times of need.

I invite you into my successes and into my messes.
I invite you into my relationships and into every time I trip.
I invite you into my pain and I invite you to remain.

Truth is - you have been and are there for it all anyway.

Holy Spirit, this week...this day...this hour...this minute...

I AM LISTENING.

Lord, what are our priorities today? _____

_____

_____

_____

Who are we praying for? _____

_____

_____

_____

What truth do you have for me today, Lord? _____

_____

_____

_____

What do I need to let go of? _____

_____

_____

_____

What do I need to receive? _____

_____

_____

_____

Lord, how can I partner with you today? _____

_____

_____

Today I am grateful for _____

_____

_____

_____

I see God In _____

_____

_____

_____

7 Am Listening - A Prayer

Holy Spirit,

You are welcome here.
I believe you care about me and long to comfort me.
I need your loving guidance in my life; I can't do it on my own.

I praise God that He designed it this way; Him, the Father,
the giver of life, His son, Jesus, imparted to set us free, and you,
the Holy Spirit, to be an ever-present help in times of need.

I invite you into my successes and into my messes.
I invite you into my relationships and into every time I trip.
I invite you into my pain and I invite you to remain.

Truth is - you have been and are there for it all anyway.

Holy Spirit, this week...this day...this hour...this minute...

I AM LISTENING.

Lord, what are our priorities today? _____

_____

_____

_____

Who are we praying for? _____

_____

_____

_____

What truth do you have for me today, Lord? _____

_____

_____

_____

What do I need to let go of? _____

_____

_____

_____

What do I need to receive? _____

_____

_____

_____

Lord, how can I partner with you today? _____

_____

_____

Today I am grateful for _____

_____

_____

_____

I see God In _____

_____

_____

_____

I Am Listening - A Prayer

Holy Spirit,

You are welcome here.
I believe you care about me and long to comfort me.
I need your loving guidance in my life; I can't do it on my own.

I praise God that He designed it this way; Him, the Father,
the giver of life, His son, Jesus, imparted to set us free, and you,
the Holy Spirit, to be an ever-present help in times of need.

I invite you into my successes and into my messes.
I invite you into my relationships and into every time I trip.
I invite you into my pain and I invite you to remain.

Truth is - you have been and are there for it all anyway.

Holy Spirit, this week...this day...this hour...this minute...

I AM LISTENING.

Lord, what are our priorities today? _____

_____

_____

_____

Who are we praying for? _____

_____

_____

_____

What truth do you have for me today, Lord? _____

_____

_____

_____

What do I need to let go of? _____

_____

_____

_____

What do I need to receive? _____

_____

_____

_____

Lord, how can I partner with you today? _____

_____

_____

Date ____ / ____ / ____

Today I am grateful for _____

_____

_____

_____

I see God In _____

_____

_____

_____

I Am Listening - A Prayer

Holy Spirit,

You are welcome here.
I believe you care about me and long to comfort me.
I need your loving guidance in my life; I can't do it on my own.

I praise God that He designed it this way; Him, the Father,
the giver of life, His son, Jesus, imparted to set us free, and you,
the Holy Spirit, to be an ever-present help in times of need.

I invite you into my successes and into my messes.
I invite you into my relationships and into every time I trip.
I invite you into my pain and I invite you to remain.

Truth is - you have been and are there for it all anyway.

Holy Spirit, this week...this day...this hour...this minute...

I AM LISTENING.

Lord, what are our priorities today? _____

_____

_____

_____

Who are we praying for? _____

_____

_____

_____

What truth do you have for me today, Lord? _____

_____

_____

_____

What do I need to let go of? _____

_____

_____

_____

What do I need to receive? _____

_____

_____

_____

Lord, how can I partner with you today? _____

_____

_____

Weekly Reflections

Did any themes emerge in your listening this week? What are the ways you saw God? Evidence the Holy Spirit is growing you? Anything else you want to remember from the week?

_____

_____

_____

_____

_____

_____

_____

_____

_____

_____

_____

_____

_____

_____

_____

_____

_____

_____

_____

_____

_____

MAY THE GOD
OF HOPE
FILL YOU WITH
all joy and peace
AS YOU TRUST
IN HIM, SO THAT YOU
MAY OVERFLOW
WITH HOPE BY THE
POWER OF THE
Holy Spirit.

ROMANS 15:13 NIV

Today I am grateful for _____

_____

_____

_____

I see God In _____

_____

_____

_____

I Am Listening - A Prayer

Holy Spirit,

You are welcome here.
I believe you care about me and long to comfort me.
I need your loving guidance in my life; I can't do it on my own.

I praise God that He designed it this way; Him, the Father,
the giver of life, His son, Jesus, imparted to set us free, and you,
the Holy Spirit, to be an ever-present help in times of need.

I invite you into my successes and into my messes.
I invite you into my relationships and into every time I trip.
I invite you into my pain and I invite you to remain.

Truth is - you have been and are there for it all anyway.

Holy Spirit, this week...this day...this hour...this minute...

I AM LISTENING.

Lord, what are our priorities today? _____

_____

_____

_____

Who are we praying for? _____

_____

_____

_____

What truth do you have for me today, Lord? _____

_____

_____

_____

What do I need to let go of? _____

_____

_____

_____

What do I need to receive? _____

_____

_____

_____

Lord, how can I partner with you today? _____

_____

_____

Today I am grateful for _____

_____

_____

_____

I see God In _____

_____

_____

_____

7 Am Listening - A Prayer

Holy Spirit,

You are welcome here.
I believe you care about me and long to comfort me.
I need your loving guidance in my life; I can't do it on my own.

I praise God that He designed it this way; Him, the Father,
the giver of life, His son, Jesus, imparted to set us free, and you,
the Holy Spirit, to be an ever-present help in times of need.

I invite you into my successes and into my messes.
I invite you into my relationships and into every time I trip.
I invite you into my pain and I invite you to remain.

Truth is - you have been and are there for it all anyway.

Holy Spirit, this week...this day...this hour...this minute...

I AM LISTENING.

Lord, what are our priorities today?

Who are we praying for?

What truth do you have for me today, Lord?

What do I need to let go of?

What do I need to receive?

Lord, how can I partner with you today?

Today I am grateful for _____

_____

_____

_____

I see God In _____

_____

_____

_____

I Am Listening - A Prayer

Holy Spirit,

You are welcome here.
I believe you care about me and long to comfort me.
I need your loving guidance in my life; I can't do it on my own.

I praise God that He designed it this way; Him, the Father,
the giver of life, His son, Jesus, imparted to set us free, and you,
the Holy Spirit, to be an ever-present help in times of need.

I invite you into my successes and into my messes.
I invite you into my relationships and into every time I trip.
I invite you into my pain and I invite you to remain.

Truth is - you have been and are there for it all anyway.

Holy Spirit, this week...this day...this hour...this minute...

I AM LISTENING.

Lord, what are our priorities today? _____

_____

_____

_____

Who are we praying for? _____

_____

_____

_____

What truth do you have for me today, Lord? _____

_____

_____

_____

What do I need to let go of? _____

_____

_____

_____

What do I need to receive? _____

_____

_____

_____

Lord, how can I partner with you today? _____

_____

_____

Today I am grateful for _____

_____

_____

_____

I see God In _____

_____

_____

_____

I Am Listening - A Prayer

Holy Spirit,

You are welcome here.
I believe you care about me and long to comfort me.
I need your loving guidance in my life; I can't do it on my own.

I praise God that He designed it this way; Him, the Father,
the giver of life, His son, Jesus, imparted to set us free, and you,
the Holy Spirit, to be an ever-present help in times of need.

I invite you into my successes and into my messes.
I invite you into my relationships and into every time I trip.
I invite you into my pain and I invite you to remain.

Truth is - you have been and are there for it all anyway.

Holy Spirit, this week...this day...this hour...this minute...

I AM LISTENING.

Lord, what are our priorities today? _____

_____

_____

_____

Who are we praying for? _____

_____

_____

_____

What truth do you have for me today, Lord? _____

_____

_____

_____

What do I need to let go of? _____

_____

_____

_____

What do I need to receive? _____

_____

_____

_____

Lord, how can I partner with you today? _____

_____

_____

Today I am grateful for _____

_____

_____

_____

I see God In _____

_____

_____

_____

I Am Listening - A Prayer

Holy Spirit,

You are welcome here.
I believe you care about me and long to comfort me.
I need your loving guidance in my life; I can't do it on my own.

I praise God that He designed it this way; Him, the Father,
the giver of life, His son, Jesus, imparted to set us free, and you,
the Holy Spirit, to be an ever-present help in times of need.

I invite you into my successes and into my messes.
I invite you into my relationships and into every time I trip.
I invite you into my pain and I invite you to remain.

Truth is - you have been and are there for it all anyway.

Holy Spirit, this week...this day...this hour...this minute...

I AM LISTENING.

Lord, what are our priorities today? _____

_____

_____

_____

Who are we praying for? _____

_____

_____

_____

What truth do you have for me today, Lord? _____

_____

_____

_____

What do I need to let go of? _____

_____

_____

_____

What do I need to receive? _____

_____

_____

_____

Lord, how can I partner with you today? _____

_____

_____

Weekly Reflections

Did any themes emerge in your listening this week? What are the ways you saw God? Evidence the Holy Spirit is growing you? Anything else you want to remember from the week?

_____

_____

_____

_____

_____

_____

_____

_____

_____

_____

_____

_____

_____

_____

_____

_____

_____

_____

_____

_____

_____

BUT THE ADVOCATE, THE *Holy Spirit,* WHOM THE FATHER WILL SEND IN MY NAME, WILL *teach you all things* AND WILL REMIND YOU OF EVERYTHING I HAVE SAID TO YOU.

1 CORINTHIANS 3:16 NIV

PAST 40 DAYS AT-A-GLANCE

I have an abundance of gratitude for

I saw God in

Our priorities included

Prayers were spoken over

Overarching truths God spoke to me

I let go of _____

_____

_____

_____

I received _____

_____

_____

_____

I partnered with the Lord when _____

_____

_____

_____

Holy Spirit,

Thank you for your loving guidance.
Thank you for showing up for me each and every day,
in big and small ways.

This week...this day...this hour...this minute...

I AM LISTENING.

ABOUT THE AUTHOR

Living in God's freedom on her first visit to Wadi Rum, Jordan.

Tammy did not grow up knowing the Lord. That all changed when the idol she made of her husband came tumbling down and their marriage was at stake. When nothing else was working to bring solace and her life was literally on the line, it was then she decided to give God a try. "Lord, if you're real, show me." Did He ever. Even to a young punk girl who was sassy and doubtful. He showed up in a mighty way and transformed her heart and marriage from the inside out. It was her faith in God that helped her heal from disordered eating, debilitating anxiety, and depression, to name a few. God was equipping her with the mental freedom and spiritual strength to start stepping into dreams He'd placed within her. Along this journey, not only did her confidence in God and belief in His word awaken, likewise, her passion for sharing the life-changing love of Christ swelled. Bible studies were born; gathering women from all faiths and no faith to learn more about this friend named Jesus. Tammy began teaching, speaking, and leading more and more to the freedom found at the feet of Jesus. She currently resides in Indiana with her high school sweetheart (praise God!), where they have been able to share the love of Christ with many through B Present, a boutique fitness studio created in faith. Both have a passion for learning about God's creation all over the world and are involved in the fight against human trafficking.

Coming Soon!

Another great resource is headed your way! Tammy has been having a blast partnering with God to design and develop a 40 day devotional that will continue to help you listen and hear from God. This devo will be the perfect partner to the journal you hold in your hands. Get ready for real-life stories you can relate to that will draw you closer to the Lord and leave you seeking His voice.

Friends,

God is near. He is here. In us. With us. Working through us. I am so glad to be on this journey with you.

xo,

Tammy

Made in the USA
Columbia, SC
08 March 2020